Butterflies

Heather Kissock

Go to **www.av2books.com**, and enter this book's unique code.

BOOK CODE

Q769325

AV² by Weigl brings you media enhanced books that support active learning.

AV² provides enriched content that supplements and complements this book. Weigl's AV² books strive to create inspired learning and engage young minds in a total learning experience.

Your AV² Media Enhanced books come alive with...

Audio
Listen to sections of the book read aloud.

Video
Watch informative video clips.

Embedded Weblinks
Gain additional information for research.

Try This!
Complete activities and hands-on experiments.

Key Words
Study vocabulary, and complete a matching word activity.

Quizzes
Test your knowledge.

Slide Show
View images and captions, and prepare a presentation.

... and much, much more!

Published by AV² by Weigl
350 5th Avenue, 59th Floor New York, NY 10118
Website: www.av2books.com

Copyright ©2018 AV² by Weigl
All rights reserved. No part of this publication may be reproduced, stored in a retrieval system, or transmitted in any form or by any means, electronic, mechanical, photocopying, recording, or otherwise, without the prior written permission of Weigl Publishers Inc.

Library of Congress Cataloging-in-Publication Data
Names: Kissock, Heather, author.
Title: Butterflies / Heather Kissock.
Description: New York, NY : AV2 by Weigl, 2016. | Series: Little backyard animals | Includes index.
Identifiers: LCCN 2016043960 (print) | LCCN 2016044408 (ebook) | ISBN 9781489653932 (hard cover : alk. paper) | ISBN 9781489653949 (soft cover : alk. paper) | ISBN 9781489653956 (Multi-user ebk.)
Subjects: LCSH: Butterflies--Juvenile literature.
Classification: LCC QL544.2 .K57 2016 (print) | LCC QL544.2 (ebook) | DDC 595.78/9--dc23
LC record available at https://lccn.loc.gov/2016043960

Printed in the United States of America in Brainerd, Minnesota
1 2 3 4 5 6 7 8 9 0 20 19 18 17 16

102016
100716

Project Coordinator: Heather Kissock
Designer: Terry Paulhus

Every reasonable effort has been made to trace ownership and to obtain permission to reprint copyright material. The publisher would be pleased to have any errors or omissions brought to its attention so that they may be corrected in subsequent printings.

The publisher acknowledges Getty and Alamy as the primary image suppliers for this title.

little backyard animals

Butterflies

In this book, I will tell you about their

home   food

family

and how they grow up.

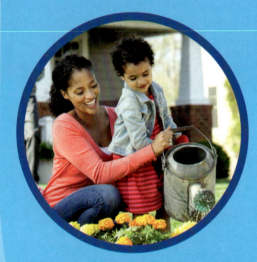

One day, I was helping my mom in the garden. She called me over to look at something.

I looked at the leaf she was holding. There was a little white ball stuck to it.

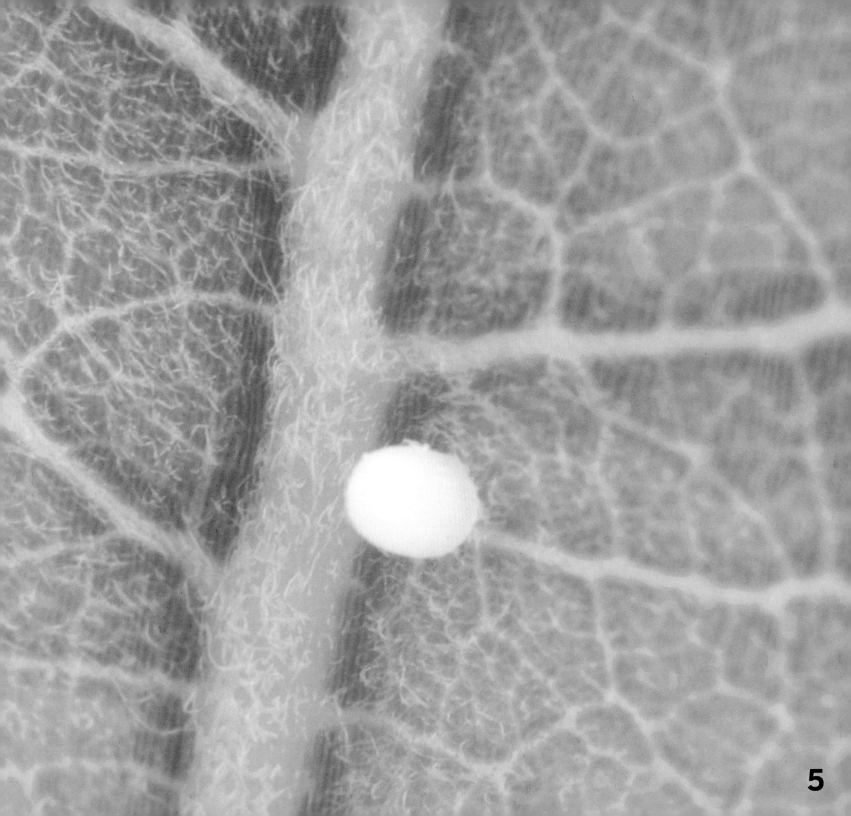

My mom said it was a butterfly egg. She told me not to touch it.

If we left the egg alone, it would grow to be a butterfly.

A few days later, I went out to the garden. The egg was not there anymore.

The leaf now had a bunch of holes in it.

My mom told me that the egg was now a caterpillar. It was eating the leaves for food. This helped it grow.

She said that the caterpillar would stop eating when it stopped growing.

I went out to the garden every now and then to find the caterpillar.

One day, I found it hanging upside down on a plant. Its head was turning green.

My mom said that the caterpillar was entering the pupa stage. This stage helps it become a butterfly.

She told me that all of the caterpillar would soon be green.

I checked on the caterpillar every day. Before long, it was covered with a hard shell. I asked my mom what the shell did.

She said that the shell kept the caterpillar safe while it changed into a butterfly.

The shell was green at first. The next time I saw it, the shell was clear. I could see something inside it.

My mom told me that the shell often turns clear the day before the butterfly comes out.

I went to the garden as soon as I got up the next day. I could see the butterfly starting to come out of the shell.

Its wings were all wrinkled at first. Then, the butterfly began flapping them. The wings became full and flat. The butterfly soon flew away.

I spent the rest of the summer looking for more eggs.

I wanted to see another butterfly grow up.

KEY WORDS

Research has shown that as much as 65 percent of all written material published in English is made up of 300 words. These 300 words cannot be taught using pictures or learned by sounding them out. They must be recognized by sight. This book contains 81 common sight words to help young readers improve their reading fluency and comprehension. This book also teaches young readers several important content words, such as proper nouns. These words are paired with pictures to aid in learning and improve understanding.

Page	Sight Words First Appearance
4	a, at, day, I, in, it, little, look, me, my, on, one, over, she, something, the, there, to, was, white
7	be, grow, if, left, not, said, we, would
9	few, had, later, now, of, out, went
10	food, for, leaves, stop, that, this, when
13	and, down, every, find, found, head, its, plant, then
15	all, helps, soon
16	asked, before, did, hard, into, long, what, while, with
19	comes, could, first, next, often, saw, see, time, turns
20	as, away, began, got, them, up, were
22	more
23	another

Page	Content Words First Appearance
4	ball, garden, leaf, mom
7	butterfly, egg
9	holes
10	caterpillar
15	pupa stage
16	shell
20	wings
22	summer

Check out www.av2books.com for activities, videos, audio clips, and more!

 Go to www.av2books.com.

 Enter book code.   Q769325

 Fuel your imagination online!

www.av2books.com